Celebrating Summer

By Rita Kohn

Illustrated by Kevin Warren Smith

The Woodland Adventures series
is dedicated to all The Woodland People
who persevere despite hardships, inhumanity, and hostility.
Their spirit, like the Eagle, soars.
Their integrity, like the Turtle, persists.

This book is dedicated to
Brian, Allen, and Kevin
who live in the Kankakee Valley.

Special thanks to:
Wap Shing, spiritual Leader of the Miami of Indiana,
and to my Consultants
Curtis Zunigha – Lenape (Delaware) and Isleta Pueblo,
Gwen Yeaman (Meda Kikalakaniqua) – Chippewa/Penobscot,
Robin McBride Scott – Cherokee,
and Beth Kohn, Early Childhood Specialist

Kohn, Rita T.
    Celebrating summer / by Rita Kohn; Illustrated by Kevin Warren
Smith.
       p. cm. – (Woodland adventures)
    ISBN 0-516-05201-2
    1. Indians of North America – Great Lakes Region – Rites and
ceremonies – Juvenile literature. 2. Indians of North America – Great
Lakes Region – Social life and customs – Juvenile literature.
3. Powwows – Great Lakes Region – Juvenile literature. 4. Summer-
-Great Lakes Region – Juvenile literature. [1. Indians of North
America – Great Lakes Region. 2. Powwows. 3. Counting. 4. Summer.]
I. Smith, Kevin Warren, ill. II. Title. III. Series.
E78.G7K63 1995
394.2 ' 63 ' 089973–dc20
                                            94-37048
                                              CIP
                                              AC

Project Editor: Alice Flanagan
Design and Electronic Production:
    PCI Design Group, San Antonio, Texas
Engraver: Liberty Photoengravers
Printer: Lake Book Manufacturing, Inc.

1 2 3 4 5 6 7 8 9 10 R 04 03 02 01 00 99 98 97 96 95

The Purpose of This Book

Celebrating Summer, one of four books
having a SEASONAL theme in the
Woodland Adventures series, is a
picture book for preschool and primary
grades based on learning to identify and
count NUMBERS ONE THROUGH TEN.

The story takes place in the summer in
a woodland region along the Great Lakes
of North America, the traditional homeland
for more than twenty NATIVE AMERICAN
nations. It focuses on one of their
annual traditions – The Woodland
Traditional POWWOW. By counting how
many dancers participate in the building of
the powwow arbor (dance arena) and what
items the dancers wear or carry in the
ceremonial dance, children strengthen
their counting skills and learn
about another culture.

 dancers gather to build a powwow arbor.
Each brings a part.

One goes away to get the .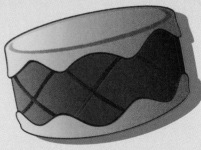

That leaves 9 dancers to raise the center pole.

One goes away to get the *drumsticks*.

That leaves 8 dancers to set the poles around.

One goes away to get her **belt**.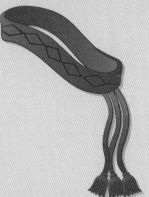

9

That leaves 7 dancers to brace the circle.

One goes away to get his *gourd*.

That leaves **6** dancers to lay the rafters.

One goes away to get her .

That leaves 5 dancers to web the roof.

14

One goes away to get his 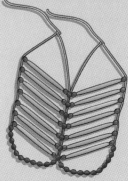 breastplate.

That leaves 4 dancers to haul the boughs.

One goes away to get her **leggings**.

That leaves 3 dancers to intertwine the boughs.

One goes away to get his **feather bustle**.

hat leaves **2** dancers to set the drummers' seats.

One goes away to get his *headdress*.

That leaves **1** dancer to announce:

"Take your places for the **POWWOW** to begin!"

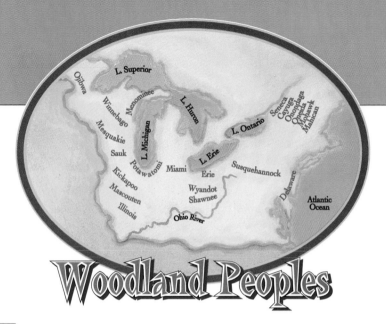

Woodland Peoples

The traditional homeland of the People of the Great Lakes woodland has many rivers and lakes and, originally, was filled with forests and grasslands. Here lived the Five Nations of the League of the Iroquois – the Mohawk, Oneida, Onondaga, Cayuga, and Seneca; and the individual Nations including the Huron, Wyandot, Ottawa, Ojibwa (commonly called Chippewa), Menominee, Dakota, Mesquakie (commonly called Fox), Sauk, Winnebago, Potawatomi, Kickapoo, Mascouten, Miami, and Shawnee.

When the Atlantic Ocean coastal region was settled by Europeans, many Indians who lived there moved to the Great Lakes region. They include the Mahican, Munsi, Lenape (commonly called Delaware), Nanticoke, Piscataway, and Osage.

British treaties giving native peoples the right to live peacefully for all time in the Great Lakes region were not honored by the government of the United States of America. By 1840, land occupied by native people living closest to the Ohio River was taken away.

The Powwow

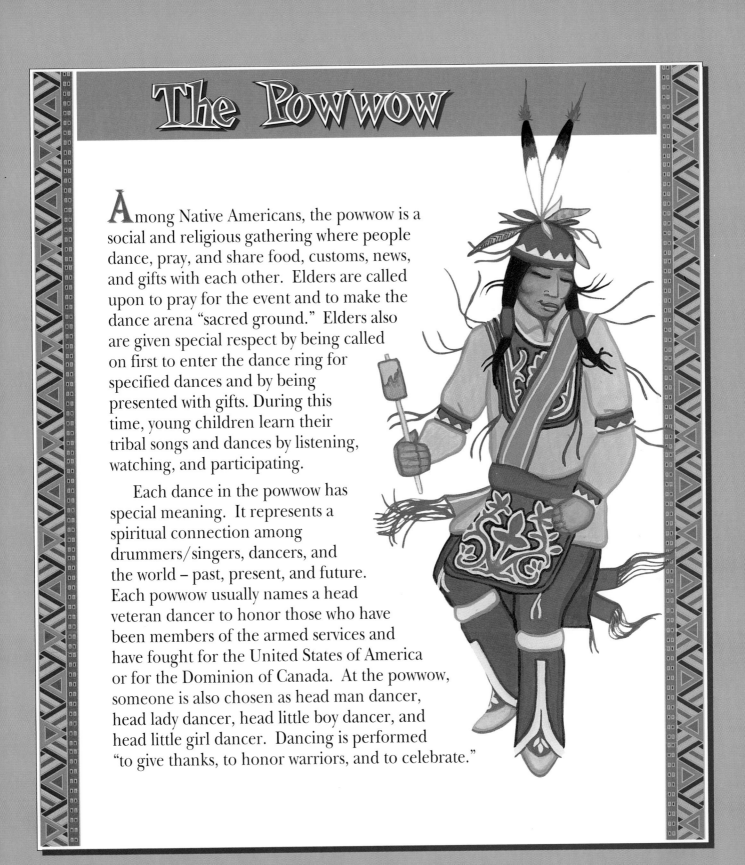

Among Native Americans, the powwow is a social and religious gathering where people dance, pray, and share food, customs, news, and gifts with each other. Elders are called upon to pray for the event and to make the dance arena "sacred ground." Elders also are given special respect by being called on first to enter the dance ring for specified dances and by being presented with gifts. During this time, young children learn their tribal songs and dances by listening, watching, and participating.

Each dance in the powwow has special meaning. It represents a spiritual connection among drummers/singers, dancers, and the world – past, present, and future. Each powwow usually names a head veteran dancer to honor those who have been members of the armed services and have fought for the United States of America or for the Dominion of Canada. At the powwow, someone is also chosen as head man dancer, head lady dancer, head little boy dancer, and head little girl dancer. Dancing is performed "to give thanks, to honor warriors, and to celebrate."

The dancers move in a circle around the arbor. A circle is the spiritual symbol of Indians of the North American continent. It represents continuity and connectedness. It is symbolic of the "circle of life," a spiritual philosophy shared by all Native Americans.

Powwow songs are handed down from generation to generation and represent the stories of the tribe. When new events require the addition of a story, the drummer/singer learns another song. Intertribal songs and dances, which are often shared, usually take the form of social dances.

Ceremonial Dance Items

Traditional clothing is worn by all participants. Typically, children are given traditional powwow clothing. However, as soon as they can, they make their own traditional clothing according to custom. Among Woodland People currently living in the Great Lakes region, there has been a return to the traditions commonly practiced by their ancestors prior to their removal from the states of Ohio, Indiana, and Illinois. Among Woodland People now living on reservations, or whose families were removed to areas west of the Mississippi River, we find more evidence of shared patterns and designs from other Native American traditions. Sometimes, a dancer might even wear something given as a gift from another tribe.

Even though each tribe has its own heritage, several universal beliefs are held by all. A sense of oneness with the world is one such belief. Respect for all the gifts of Mother Earth and Father Sky means that nothing is wasted or taken for granted. When a four-legged, a winged, or a swimmer is to be killed for food, permission is sought from the creature. Then, thanks are given after the creature has given up its life. In honor of the creature, something from it (such as a claw, a feather, a bone, or a horn) is attached to clothing worn for a powwow.

Dance items have special meaning for each dancer and may have several useful purposes beyond their ornamental nature.

Ceremonial Dance Items

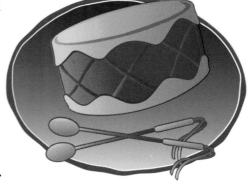

The drum, which is one of the most important items in the powwow, symbolizes the human heartbeat. There are special drums for each use within the life cycles of the tribe. The large dance drum, around which several drummers and singers sit, is for powwows only and is not used for other ceremonies. The making of a drum is sacred and requires special teaching. Drumsticks are made by wrapping animal hide around the ends of sturdy sticks.

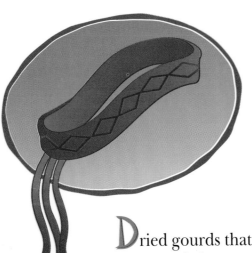

A finger-woven sash or belt may be handed down from a grandmother, and thus tells a family story.

Dried gourds that have been made into rattles often accompany the drum. Some are used as containers from which dancers can drink water.

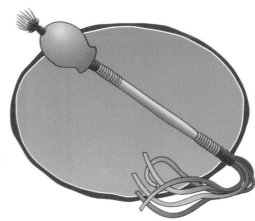

Ceremonial Dance Items

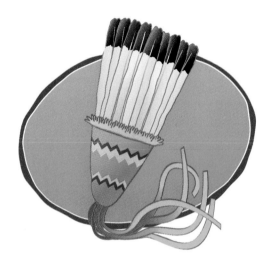

A fan of feathers, which may represent gifts from many people, is often used to cool off dancers.

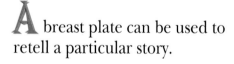

A breast plate can be used to retell a particular story.

Leggings, which go to the knee on women and extend to the hips on men, are distinct for each tribe and region.

Ceremonial Dance Items

The feather bustle, which is worn only for dancing, is part of the story told by the dancer.

The Woodland roach headdress is made from porcupine hair and deer tail hair. Eagle feathers, which are connected to the center of the headdress, must be earned.

Powwow clothing connects the wearer to his or her own personal history, to a particular tribal history, and to the relationship each person has to the world.

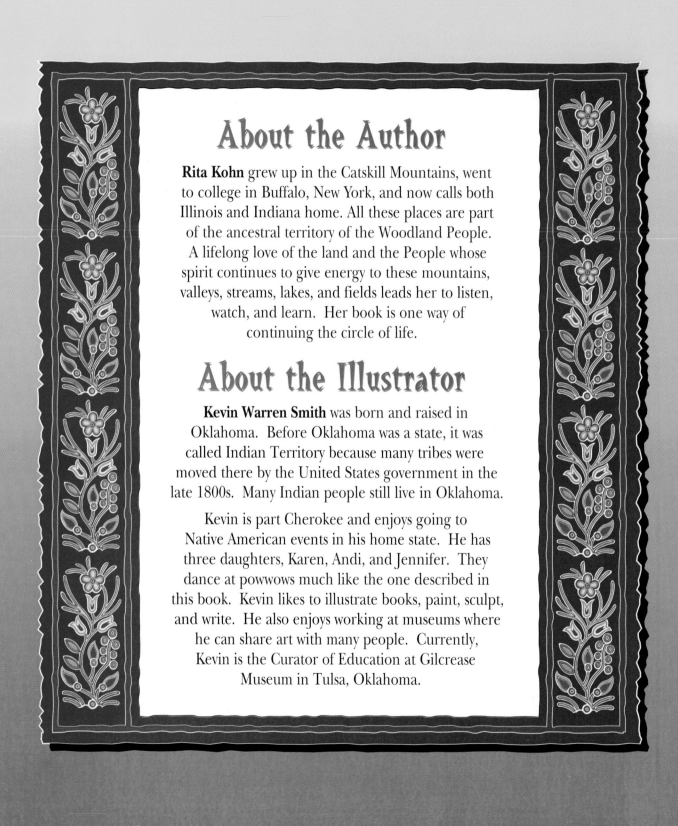

About the Author

Rita Kohn grew up in the Catskill Mountains, went to college in Buffalo, New York, and now calls both Illinois and Indiana home. All these places are part of the ancestral territory of the Woodland People. A lifelong love of the land and the People whose spirit continues to give energy to these mountains, valleys, streams, lakes, and fields leads her to listen, watch, and learn. Her book is one way of continuing the circle of life.

About the Illustrator

Kevin Warren Smith was born and raised in Oklahoma. Before Oklahoma was a state, it was called Indian Territory because many tribes were moved there by the United States government in the late 1800s. Many Indian people still live in Oklahoma.

Kevin is part Cherokee and enjoys going to Native American events in his home state. He has three daughters, Karen, Andi, and Jennifer. They dance at powwows much like the one described in this book. Kevin likes to illustrate books, paint, sculpt, and write. He also enjoys working at museums where he can share art with many people. Currently, Kevin is the Curator of Education at Gilcrease Museum in Tulsa, Oklahoma.